SAM PLAYS HIDE AND SEEK

Green Fig

A Green Fig Book
Illustrated by Yara Mahdi

Name :

Note To Parents

God created the six directions: up, down, right, left, in front of, and behind. Direction is defined as the place of an object relative to something else. Since direction is relative and created, it applies only to the created bodies, and is not befitting to attribute to God, the Creator of the bodies. That God exists, without existing in a place or a direction is one of the fundamental tenets of Islam. *Sam Plays Hide and Seek* was written as a way to introduce the concept of direction to children and to reinforce to them that God exists without being in a direction.

Everything that is in a direction is a body—whether it is a 'thin' body (that which cannot be grasped by the hand) or a 'thick' body (that which might be grasped by the hand). Light, darkness, and wind are examples of the thin bodies which occupy space and have a place. The stars, the moon, and the sun are examples of thick bodies which occupy space and are in a place. The stars, the moon, and the sun are in the space (a distance of 500 years) between our earth and the first sky, a solid body 500 years thick. So, they are in the direction of 'above' in relation to us, and in the direction of 'below' in relation to the first sky.

It is important to teach your children that the angels inhabit the skies, and that God does not occupy the skies or any other place. Teach your children not to ask, "Where is God?" because this question is only for created things that have directions relative to each other. Protect your children by teaching them the correct belief in God before they encounter the blasphemous teachings of misguided factions who say that God is in the sky, or God sits on the Throne, or God surrounds us in all directions (like the air) or God is in everything, among other blasphemous sayings. Teach them to reject anything that contradicts *Ayah* 11 of *Suratush-Shura*, (لَيْسَ كَمِثْلِهِ شَـىْءٌ), the most explicit verse in the Qur'an clearing God from any attribute of the creation. It means: Nothing resembles Him (God) in any way.

We ask God that this book benefits in teaching and spreading the correct belief.

The authors,
Rola and Sue

Sam loves to play hide and seek.
It is his favorite game.

Sam finds very clever places to hide
and his mom has to search in
all the directions to find him.

She covers her eyes, counts to 10, then shouts,

"Ready or not,
here I come."

Let's look for Sam.

Is Sam sitting
above the playhouse?

No, two blue pigeons
are resting there.

Is Sam below the porch table?

No, his red firetruck
is forgotten there.

Is Sam squeezing
to the right of the refrigerator?

No, a big bag of potatoes
is stored there.

Is Sam crouching
to the left of the bed?

No, his school backpack
is lying there.

Is Sam sitting
in front of the TV?

No, his little brother
is watching cartoons there.

Is Sam standing behind
the laundry room door?

No, an old broom
is hanging there.

Hmmmm...... Where is Sam?

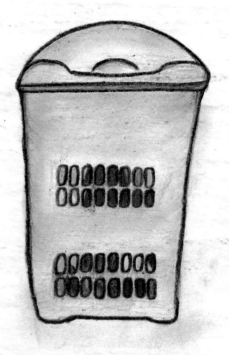

"Here I am mom."

Above and below.

Right and left.

In front of and behind.

These are the six directions.

God created all the directions.

God is not in any direction.

**Encourage your child to memorize the saying of
Imam Abu Ja^far at-Tahawiyy:**

لا تحويه الجهات الست كسائر المبتدعات

Lā tahwīhil jihātus-sittu kasā'iril-mubtada^āt
**(The six directions do not contain Him,
whereas directions contain the created things.)**

It means:
**God is clear of existing in a direction.
It is the created things which exist in the six directions.**

The *Proud Muslim Kids* series by *Green Fig* books is designed to engagingly teach youngsters basic concepts of Islam in a way that speaks to their hearts and minds. Each book in the series is crafted by a staff of qualified educators, writers, illustrators, parents and children. Not only is the *Proud Muslim Kids* series designed to supplement the early childhood and elementary Islamic curriculum, it is a great addition to any school or home library. Covering a wide variety of topics such as the Five Pillars of Islam, Islamic culture, and Islamic history, parents and children will return to these books and enjoy them together time and time again.

Green Fig